MW00414990

IF IT AIN'T BROKE,

Break It

A Spiritual Guide
Through the Process of Transition

DR. CHRIS BOWEN

If It Ain't Broke, Break It: A Spiritual Guide Through the Process of Transition

by Dr. Chris Bowen, D.Min

copyright ©2019 Chris Bowen

ISBN: 978-1-950718-10-8

published by Dream Releaser Publishing

cover design by Kiryl Lisenko

If It Ain't Broke, Break It is available in Amazon Kindle, Barnes & Noble Nook and Apple iBooks.

Contents

FOREWORD

F OR OVER TWO DECADES, Dr. Chris Bowen has called me "Mother." At first, my response was, "Christopher Scott Bowen, I am not your mother. I am too young to be your mother. I could be your older sister, maybe, but not your mother." You see, I was 40ish, and he was 30ish. At that age, I wasn't thinking "spiritual mother." It was a busy stage of life for me. I had no intentions of having spiritual offspring.

I've known Chris since he was a teenager, and his wife, Kathy, since she was in elementary school. My husband and I were Kathy's pastors, and my husband officiated their wedding.

Fast-forward a decade from the wedding: Chris and Kathy started a church in the most poverty-stricken, crime-ridden area of Atlanta. During their tenure, Kathy once held a young gunshot victim in her arms, in the church parking lot, as he transitioned from this life.

In the beginning, the couple purchased an old convenience store and converted it into a church. The two walk-in coolers became classrooms. In time, they acquired adjoining property and converted it into offices. That campus became a hub of activity. Chris hosted events, they conducted outreach, and they fed thousands of people each week who lived in the apartment complexes surrounding the church. Eventually, Chris acquired a large piece of property and built a remarkable complex within a mile of the original campus.

Chris and Kathy had experienced incredible miracles to reach that point in their ministry. As a professor of leadership courses at Beulah Heights University, I asked him to teach as a visiting instructor to inspire my students. Chris would tell them the stories of his accomplishments. I would go down the list: *Tell them the story of standing in the bank when you closed on the property.* (He didn't have money to close, but was so convinced it would be there that he kept going to the bank and asking the teller to check his account. When the money came in, the teller rushed to meet him in the lobby, saying, "It's here!") *Tell them the chandelier story!* (He acquired a $25,000 chandelier for the church foyer for $5,000.) *Tell them about the businessman who sent you a check for $150,000 with a thank you for building such a beautiful edifice in the community. Tell them the one about ...* I didn't want him to leave anything out. The students needed to hear it all.

I don't know why I felt I had the liberty to walk into his church office one day and tell him, "You need to go back to school and get your master's degree." I am not certain how I had the audacity. It was not, and still isn't, my nature to address anyone in that manner. Then, later, I told him he needed to go on to get his doctorate. He is currently the director of our coaching program, and I asked him to become credentialed with the premier coaching agency in the business. He accomplished that. The latest thing I asked him to do was to become certified to administer personality testing. At this writing, my request is pending but on the schedule, and we expect to add it to the accomplished list soon.

The odds were against Chris achieving all that he has. He grew up in extreme poverty. His life was filled with domestic violence, as well as mental, physical, and emotional abuse. The public school system was another negative environment for him. Instead of encouraging him to press through learning disabilities such as attention deficit disorder, this environment pegged him as someone incapable of learning—someone to simply be shoved through the system. During his formative years, he was treated as someone who would not amount to anything. Many thought he had low odds of making it in the world. However, they underestimated the tenacity, resilience, and determination (not to mention the God factor) of this Energizer bunny (actually, the Energizer bunny is slow compared to Chris).

Fast-forward again to today. Chris is 50ish, and I am 60ish (closing in on 70ish). Today, I am intentional, and embrace the concept of being a spiritual mother (Why not ride that tide? I am often the oldest person in the room, anyway.) Being a spiritual parent is not a tough job. All you have to do is be, and share, who you are. Years ago, I came up with my vision statement: "When I become aware, I must share through teaching, mentoring, coaching, and life example." I simply need to live that out.

Recently, I heard someone say that the goal of parenting is to "wean your child from your wisdom." What a great statement (I heard it as I was channel surfing, so unfortunately, I don't know who said it). My interpretation is this: You start out telling your child what to do, how to do it, and when to do it. Then, you let them make simple decisions. Ultimately, they are weaned from you telling them what to do, and they are able to make their own wise choices. The mother's voice will remain in their head like a good coach, saying, "Breathe," "Sit up straight," and so on. Before you know it, the child is on his or her own, and they have surpassed your highest expectations.

The last time I saw one of my mentors, he honored me by calling me one of his "3 John 2 children." Third John 2 reads, "For I rejoiced greatly, when the brethren came and testified of the truth that is in thee, even as thou walkest in the truth. I have no greater joy than to hear that my children walk in truth." So, Chris, I declare you a "3 John 2 child." Go, continue to fly. Continue to live your dream. And thank you for honoring me by calling me "Mother."

— Dr. Brenda Chand

chapter 1

IF IT AIN'T BROKE, BREAK IT

W E'VE ALL HEARD THE SAYING, "If it ain't broke, don't fix it." The meaning of that motto is, "If something works, leave it alone." In my opinion, that's simply a visionless person's excuse not to strive for improvement. I'm grateful for people who choose to take things that are working and find ways to make them even better.

For instance, the outhouse was not broken. People used outhouses for years, never giving them a second thought. The walk to the outhouse was the norm. People put up with flies and other critters, the smells, and everything else that was a part of the experience. Aren't you glad that Sir John Harington created the first flushing toilet? I'm thankful that, even though the outhouse worked fine, he had vision to bring it inside and add water. Harington had a greater vision for something that wasn't broken, so he broke it and made everyone's lives better.

If you know anything about farming, you know that you can't harvest where the ground isn't broken. If soil is hard and unfertile, it won't produce an effective harvest. The ground must be broken, turned, and properly tilled in order for seed to germinate and produce a crop. In the book of Jeremiah, the prophet teaches us, "Break up your unplowed ground and *do not sow among thorns*" (4:3, NIV, emphasis mine). Any successful farmer can tell you that this is not an easy task. Farmers get up before sunrise, and work until long after sunset, to reap a bountiful harvest.

It is the same with our lives. We have to decide: will we be complacent, telling ourselves that we're content with where we are now in our marriage, career, spiritual life, health, finances, and family? Or will we do the work required to take those things to the next level? Even if you currently feel satisfied with where you are, just like Sir John Harington, you should realize there is always a way to improve, and break, what seems unbroken! Maybe you have a great marriage; be creative, and invent ways to make it stronger.

Anything you value must go through transition. Nothing stays the same forever. What was once new becomes worn. What was young becomes old, and what was vibrant becomes dull. Hence, transition is essential. As I've traveled the globe, I've discovered this: when churches, organizations, or businesses say, "We've never done it this way before," that is a sign of death. Anything not growing is dying. We must be willing to do things as they have never been done before.

There are some things in our lives that may not be broken; however, we need to consider breaking them. What are some of those things? How about our attitude, hatred, anger, jealousy, or pride? There is always room for improvement.

"Any transition is easier if you believe in yourself and your talent." —Priyanka Chopra

---

Transition doesn't have to be resisted. As a former pastor and current life coach, my greatest joy is helping people get unstuck. The first thing we need to change is our mindset regarding brokenness. Being broken doesn't have to be a negative thing. Sometimes in transition, we feel that we are alone. We assume that no one else has experienced the pain, heartache, and isolation of transitioning to the next level. The Bible teaches that, when we are broken, God is close to us! Psalms 34:18 says, "The Lord is close to the brokenhearted and saves those who are crushed in spirit" (NIV).

I remember how intimidated I was when I started my educational journey. I wish I could say I was valedictorian of my high school, but that would be a huge stretch of the imagination. After graduation, I left home and traveled 600 miles to attend a Bible college. I knew nothing about the Bible. I struggled; but after four years, I received my Bachelor of Arts. It was almost 15 years later that my spiritual mother, Dr. Brenda Chand, who wrote the foreword to this book, would inspire me to go back to school. At that time, my ministry was growing, my flock was being fed, and my family was growing. *Why should I spend years in a classroom to get a master's degree?* I wondered. She would not let it go. In my mind, this wasn't broken. It was working for me! I wished she would just leave it alone. Then, one day, Brenda finally said, "In order to go where God wants you to go, you have to go back to school." She had broken something that was, in my mind, perfectly fine.

After struggling with my insecurities, I followed her instructions and went back to school to get my master's degree in leadership. It was one of the hardest decisions I have ever made, because I didn't feel like I needed it! I only went back because of my respect for her. Lo and behold, three years later, I graduated with a 4.0 grade point average. I was ecstatic. I had done what I'd felt I could never do! I had a master's degree, and the sky was the limit.

Brenda didn't even give me a weekend to celebrate before telling me I needed to go back for my doctorate. *Wait a minute,* I thought. *Now she's gone too far! Only smart people become doctors!* Well, I was wrong about that. I now know that persistent people become doctors. Again, she pushed and pushed. Finally, I agreed. It took another three years in the classroom, but I will never forget the May morning in 2011 when I walked across the stage at Oral Roberts University, at the age of 46, and they announced, for the first time, "Dr. Christopher Bowen." What a day!

You see, my life was good. I didn't need to be broken; I was already on a great path. But I must confess: Brenda was right. The doors that opened for me as I continued my education would never have opened had I not allowed her to break what was not broken. She took a young, successful pastor and created a spiritual giant. I am so thankful she was the hammer that broke my life and made me a better pastor, friend, husband, father, and person. God puts these people in our lives—people who see potential in us that we've never seen. On the other hand, Brenda didn't let up. Here I am, eight years after my doctorate, and she still has me in school. I have to laugh as we talk about it, because even though she's right, I hate to be broken so many times. Each time I further my education, it grows me to a new level. It moves me to my purpose in life. We all need someone who can break in us what has not yet been broken.

Just because we started our journey in one direction doesn't mean we can't shift into something even greater. Throughout this book, I'll discuss transitions in ministry, career, and life. This is raw content designed to help pastors, business owners, corporate leaders, and individuals who desire to live on purpose, yet feel stuck with no hope of advancing. This book will inspire your faith, feed your desire, and make you want to turn the page to the next chapter in your own personal story.

If you are living in poverty, *break it!* If you are living with an addiction, take the first step to *break it!* If you are living in fear of failure (or success), *break it!* Let's begin this journey together, walking through the steps of transition to move you to your destiny.

For Thought:

1. What can be the power of breaking something that is not broken?

2. Name at least one thing that needs to be broken in your life.

3. On a scale of 1-10, how likely are you to make the transition that needs to be made in your life?

chapter 2
TRANSITION: WHY RESIST?

TRANSITION IS THE PROCESS of changing from one state, or condition, to another. The Greek philosopher Heraclitus said, "The only thing that is constant is change." Change is not only essential; it is inevitable. It will happen, whether we like it or not. We must keep up with the times in order to succeed.

This is not a new principle. When the Wright brothers flew the first plane in 1903, a flight of 852 feet that lasted a mere 59 seconds, no one guessed where aviation would be in the twenty-first century. When Henry Ford rolled out the first Model T automobile in 1908, people never thought the fad would last. Today, nearly 1.2 billion automobiles are driven in the world, on more than 64 million miles of road.

In order to succeed in these ever-changing times, we need to shift to a positive perspective on transition. Technology has transformed our lives in ways that we never could have imagined fifty years ago. Information is at our fingertips. We can communicate, visually, with people around the world. We have a computer, phone, calculator, banking system, map, stereo, dictionary, and more, in a device that fits in the palms of our hands. In order for this to happen, someone had to think outside the box, and convince others that it was possible as well.

Why do we resist transition? As parents, we know our children go through developmental changes. They grow from infants, to toddlers, to teenagers, to adults. It would be selfish for any parent to stifle their child from these necessary transitions. As much as we would like for time to stand still, we realize it won't. Every parent has wished their children would stay young, because it's painful to let them go. However, it's essential in order for them to reach their life's purpose.

As parents, and as people in general, we realize that transition is more than change. It requires willingness to let go of what used to be and grasp what can be—all in order to grow into something bigger and better.

Managing transition makes the difficult process less painful. As Leah Busque said, "Life is like monkey bars: You have to let go in order to move forward."

One of the most beautiful examples of a true leader who realized the necessity of change is 93-year-old Jennie Mae Cain. Jennie was a precious church member, and one of my greatest supporters. She invited my family to dinner at least once a month, and we enjoyed food and great fellowship together.

One evening, after our meal, Jennie asked me to join her in the living room. She wanted to talk to me concerning a young group of rappers who had ministered at church the previous Sunday. I held my breath, sure I was about to receive a tongue-lashing about allowing that type of music on our platform. I'll never forget her words as she pointed her little crooked, arthritic finger in my face: "Now, about those young men last night. I couldn't understand a word they were saying, and I didn't like it; but I sure could feel the Spirit of the Lord in them! When can they do it again?" I thought I was going to pass out! This Caucasian, old-school saint *requested* a repeat performance of something she didn't even enjoy, simply because she knew it would draw the young people to God. I knew I was in the presence of one of the greatest leaders I would ever have the honor of knowing.

Think of your life as a drive in a vehicle. It's important to glance in your rearview mirror occasionally, to remember how you've come to be where you are. However, it's crucial to keep your focus on the windshield in order to reach your destination. Often, we're so busy looking at our past that we miss our future. As we get older, we tend to be resistant to change. After all, change takes us out of our comfort zone and creates unfamiliar challenges. We must be willing to adapt to the unknown. Instead of sitting in our rocking chairs complaining about change, we need to embrace life's transitions.

The process of transition is often complicated; but it's not impossible if you commit to staying on course. The first step to a successful transition is letting go of what used to be. This requires honest soul searching, and a willingness to admit that it's time to release it.

If you were planning on changing careers, what would you have to do differently? You might take a new course of study, get a new degree, have specialized training in the field, or make a variety of other plans for the future. You'd also lose your current occupational identity. These are the things that moving into a new career would cause you to think about.

A few years ago, I had the joy of meeting a remarkable young lady who was a student in my Success for Life class at Beulah Heights University. Her name is Keisha. Keisha entered the classroom in a wheelchair, having lost both of her legs in a car accident. Immediately, my heart went out to her. My automatic response was to feel sympathy, and empathy, for her. But within moments of our first conversation together, I was amazed and inspired by Keisha's positive outlook on her situation.

Although Keisha has endured pain and inconveniences throughout her horrific ordeal, she's discovered, in the process of recovery, just how strong she truly is. Rather than allowing herself to become isolated, or to slip into depression, self-pity, or any other understandable reaction to sorrow and loss, this incredible single mother of three quickly decided this wasn't the end of her story. She chose to make it her new beginning. Keisha shared with me that she lost her legs to find her wings!

"Learn to embrace change in your work and personal life and make the transition to a better you." —Anonymous

---

Keisha's positive outlook, and her story of overcoming odds that were stacked so high against her, has transformed her life. She shares her inspirational testimony nationally, and doors of opportunity continue to open. This woman is an awesome example of strength in the midst of tragedy. Keisha never asked for her life-altering accident. She didn't do anything to deserve it. It was out of her control. Yet, it happened. Rather than resisting the sudden changes, she made the decision to embrace the transition in the most amazing way. Her near-death experience is what caused her to truly live!

Most of us are in a transition of some kind or another. Whether it is by choice, or due to circumstances out of our control, we are in the process. The good news is that, even if unfortunate occurrences brought you to a transition, they can still result in personal growth. This transition can still propel you into your purpose!

Do you have talents or gifts that you put on the back burner? Maybe you hope to use them "someday" in the future. What if, instead, you brought these gifts to the forefront of your life now? Or maybe you were recently in a situation that made you feel unimportant or unappreciated? A transition could lead you to a place where you realize your value and regain a powerful sense of self-worth.

There are certain stages of change one must understand in order to move through transition properly. Without knowing these stages, transitions can be catastrophic to all involved. People are often uncomfortable with change, and for this reason oppose and resist it. With this in mind, the following transition model, created by William Bridges in his book *Managing Transition*, helps us understand the process of change clearly.

Bridges's model focuses on transition, not change. The difference between these two may be subtle, but it is important. Change happens to people, even if we resist it. Transition, on the other hand, is internal. It's what happens in our minds as we go through change. Change can take place very quickly, while transition usually occurs slowly.

Bridges's model highlights three stages of transition. Stage 1 includes ending, losing, and letting go. Stage 2 covers the neutral zone. Finally, Stage 3 helps us reach the new beginning. According to Bridges, individuals must go through these stages at their own pace. Those who are comfortable with change will probably advance to stage three more quickly, while others will stay in their comfort zones, in stages one or two. Let's take a look at each stage in greater detail.

Individuals enter the first stage of transition when they are presented with change. This stage is often entered into with resistance, because people are being forced to let go of something with which they are comfortable. In stage one, people may experience several emotions, including fear, frustration, denial, uncertainty, anger, sadness, disorientation, and a sense of loss. At this point, we have to accept that something is ending, before we can begin to accept the new idea. If we never acknowledge our emotions, we'll probably encounter resistance throughout the entire process.

During this stage, we must allow ourselves time to accept the change and let go. We need to have conversations about our feelings with empathetic people who listen well. People fear what they don't understand; the more you educate yourself about your future, and what knowledge and skills are an important part of getting there, the more likely you are to move on to the next stage.

Let's take a look at Stage 2: The Neutral Zone. During this stage, individuals affected by change are often confused, uncertain, and impatient. Depending on how well they manage change, they may also experience a higher workload as they get used to new systems. This phase can be seen as the bridge between the old and the new. People may still be connected to the old, but they are also trying to adapt to the new. It is during Stage 2 that people begin to feel resentment toward the change. They may experience low morale, anxiety, or even an identity crisis. It's common to become skeptical about the change process altogether.

Despite the challenges, it is in this stage that the greatest creativity, innovation, and renewal may be found. Stage 2 creates an encouragement for new ways of thinking. While it may seem that little progress is being made, this time to reflect is essential to moving forward. It's important to set short-term goals during this stage, so you can experience some quick wins.

In Stage 3, we look for the first time at a new beginning. This last stage is a time of acceptance and energy. You have begun to embrace the change initiative. You are building the skills you need to work successfully, and people are starting to see early wins in your efforts. It is in the third stage that people are likely to experience high energy, openness to learning, and fresh commitment to their new role. Make sure you take time to celebrate the change you have gone through, and reward yourself for all your hard work. Make sure, at this stage, that you don't become complacent. Remember, not everyone will reach this stage in the same amount of time. It's even possible to slide back to previous stages if you begin thinking that the change isn't working for you.

I trust that this book will inspire you to do what you once thought impossible. It is my sincere desire that we no longer fear transition, but that we see it as an opportunity to explore our destinies. Throughout the next several chapters, I'll transparently share some personal stories to inspire you to take the leap into your destiny. After all, the saddest thing is the person who's standing at the edge of changing their life forever, but climbs back into their boat of comfort.

I have found that there are "water-walkers" and "water-talkers." Which will you become? Will you keep fantasizing about what could be? Or will you reminisce on what was and what it became? Water-talkers will only talk about what they are going to do. They never leave the place of comfort, but sit comfortably around others who are content.

On the other hand, water-walkers are ready to get out of the boat and make it happen. My desire is that, through these chapters, a part of you will come to life— that you will dream again and embrace transition in your life. As long as time exists, we are all going to get older. We may fight it; but at the end of the day, change will prevail. Therefore, we have to make the best of each stage of our lives and welcome the changes that move us to the next phase.

The process of transition is not easy, but it is required to live out the dream God has destined for you. If you're ready, let's begin the journey. It all starts by not allowing ourselves to become average. Next, I am going to recreate for you the story of my own "average" period.

For Thought:

1. In what ways have you resisted transition?

2. What form of transition are you currently experiencing in your personal life?

3. What negative thought/attitude could you change to make transition a more positive experience for you?

chapter 3

WHY BE AVERAGE WHEN YOU CAN BE UNIQUE?

E HEAR THE WORD *AVERAGE* frequently in conversation. You may say, *"I'm having an average day,"* meaning your day is about normal. We may refer to people, objects, and other things as *average*. When used in mathematics, the term refers to a number that is a typical representation of a group of numbers, or data set. But what does it mean for an individual to be average?

Anyone can be average. It takes someone unique to do what no one else has done. Sometimes, we just have to take a risk! I have discovered that an individual fails seven times for every success they experience. This means that the more that you fail, the more you succeed. The only thing worse than failing is to never try at all. Cemeteries are full of people who lost hope and settled for less than their dreams. Thomas Edison said that he did not fail 10,000 times creating the light bulb; he simply found 9,999 ways that it didn't work. He never gave up! Edison had 1,093 patents for inventions. Many of these were a success and are still in use today, such as the light bulb, the motion picture camera, and the phonograph. However, the majority of his patents were failures. Yet, because of his determination, our lives are much different. He chose not to settle for being average.

Too easily, we settle for an average job, an average marriage, an average career, and an average spiritual life because it becomes familiar. What if Jerry Baldwin, Gordon Bowker, and Zev Siegl, the founders of Starbucks Coffee, had given up after being declined a loan for their company more than 200 times? The world would be different, to say the least. In every country I visit, I always find a Starbucks. Why? Because these men dared to offer something no one else had offered. Even though others didn't believe in them, they were determined not to be average.

This is why transition is so important. We can't remain stuck in the past. While we must never forget our heritage, we must also never allow it to dictate our future. If it ain't broke, break it! Stop going with the flow, and be like the salmon, which gets its strength by swimming against the current.

The truth is, we are all average. It amazes me how many people around the world are offended by this statement. As I give them a moment to ponder it, they feel insulted. "Everyone in the room is average!" I tell them. "I have been watching each of you, and I have come to the conclusion that you are all average." You can feel the negative energy flood the room. The body language shifts.

Whether we like it or not, it is true. *What are we the average of?* is the question. Are you ready for the answer? You are the average of the five people you hang around the most. Positive people like being around other positive people. Wealthy people don't want to hang around others who can never eat out, pay their own way, or afford events. People who never seem to make enough money—who rarely go to movies, and are always talking about the high price of gas—will hang around one another. It's always fun for me to hear what people are talking about—it will tell you a lot about them. Someone once told me, "I don't know why people always share gossip with me." Well, I can probably tell you! As my mother taught me, "Birds of a feather flock together." We must take notice of those around us. Are they positive, influential, and encouraging, or are they bringing us down?

As you walk through transition, it's important to have those around you who have successfully been through the journey and remain positive about the process. Otherwise, people may influence us to remain average with them, not allowing us to advance into our destiny. You must ask yourself some hard questions: *Whom do I need to cut from my life? What kind of people should I have surrounding me? Where do I find such people?* Often, we don't take the steps to surround ourselves with those who will push us to go higher. For instance, many have a goal to become a entrepreneurs, but they don't surround themselves with other entrepreneurs.

"Sometimes God brings times of transition to create transformation." —Lynn Cowell

---

The problem with becoming more than average is that it brings a lot of conflict. It often requires the loss of re-lationships. Think about the people you associate with the most. If you were to receive a promotion, or even started your own business, would they applaud you, or try to talk you out of "such nonsense"? Making this as-sessment of your close circle is difficult; but it's neces-sary to realize who is truly for you, and who isn't.

As we transition, conflict is inevitable, In Dr. Samuel Chand's manual, *Unstuck: Accelerate Your Life,* he explains how to defuse conflict. Chand uses the acronym PLUS to simplify the process. Let's take a look at it.

P - Pause: Stop whatever you're doing and focus on the situation, even if the other person is not doing so.

L - Listen: Pay attention to what the other person is saying; use body language and paraphrasing to demonstrate that you're really listening.

U - Understand: Make sure you know the real issue, validate the other person's feelings, and discuss when both parties can expect the matter to be settled. Conflict can be useful for any organization or relationship; having disagreements often produces the most creative results. However, resolutions should be carefully worked out over time. Here are six principles to follow:

1. Deal with one issue at a time.
2. Clearly define the problem.
3. Agree on the problem's definition.
4. If more than one issue is presented, agree on the order in which issues will be addressed.
5. Explore all the dimensions of the problem(s).
6. Explore several alternative solutions to the problem(s), with a response such as, "I hear you saying that..."

S- Solve - Talk about how the two of you might solve the problem. If the solution is your responsibility, tell the other person what you plan to do to resolve the issue.

Conflict will happen, but being prepared for it will help us grow from it, and use it in a positive manner. The road of transition isn't smooth; it's bumpy, and filled with unplanned detours. Most of all, it is a lonely road. The old saying, "It's lonely at the top," couldn't be truer. The process that takes you to your life's destiny is the hardest trip you will ever take. Others won't understand, and may desert you. But don't let anyone, or anything, hold you back from your purpose.

In the beginning of my pastoral career, I was constantly surrounded by people. We began with just 15 congregants, and I considered these founding members family. I attended every ball game of my members' children. I went to family reunions, helped them move to new homes, repaired their roofs, and made hospital visits to their family members. I was able to be a superhero, of sorts, to them.

As the church began to grow, however, I stretched myself too thin to keep up this pace. I could no longer attend all the birthday parties and graduations. I had to stop my free home repair business and suggest good, fair companies that could help them instead. This didn't sit well with some of my congregation. Some of my faithful members became disgruntled *former* members! This devastated me for a while. Eventually, I had to realize that, in order to grow higher and further toward your goal, you can't hang onto people or things that are holding you down. It would be like a ship trying to sail with a heavy anchor holding it down, preventing it from ever reaching its final destination.

Once a caterpillar breaks out of its cocoon, it doesn't flutter around searching for other caterpillars to hang out with—it simply flies. I'm not saying you'll lose every relationship you've ever had, but some people simply can't go with you. There's nothing wrong with them. They aren't bad people. They just can't go. It's not for them. It is for you.

I'm reminded of the story of Lot in the Bible. In Genesis 19, the angels urge Lot to grab his wife and daughters and run out of Sodom and Gomorrah before the cities are destroyed by God. In verse 17, the angels give very specific instructions: "Flee for your lives! Don't look back, and don't stop anywhere in the plain. Flee to the mountains or you will be swept away!" In verse 26, we read the tragic report that Lot's wife simply couldn't resist the urge to look back, and she became a pillar of salt.

Once you've worked up the courage to escape from the places or people keeping you from achieving your dream, don't look back! Keep your focus on what's ahead of you. I will never forget the people who helped me to different levels in my life; but I can't spend my time and energy trying to backtrack to check in on them all.

As Tyler Perry (or "Madea") taught, people in our lives can be compared to parts of a tree. Some people are the leaves; they may be acquaintances. We may meet them from time to time and carry on small talk, but there's no real relationship—they come and go quickly. Others are like branches; these people stay for a while. They are stronger than leaves. Your relationship with these individuals seems strong; but when a storm comes, they break off! Last, there are the roots. These are few and far between. Whatever comes or goes, these people are with you. You can count on them. These are the ones who not only support you on your journey, but pack up their stuff and go with you!

At this point of your journey, you may not have any "root people," but don't let that stop you. Maybe you haven't walked far enough to meet up with them yet. The road to being above average isn't a popular one; but when your dream actually becomes reality, it will be so, so worth it!

If you are the smartest person in the room, you are in the wrong room. Imagine what life would be like if you entered every room knowing that you were the best person in it. Would this fulfill you? Would this make you happy? Would this make you feel better than everyone else? Would it cause you to be complacent, and take your eyes off what's really important? The smartest person in the room is the only one incapable of learning. As the smartest person in the room, you are *it*. What comes next? How can you motivate yourself to become better in such a setting?

I've learned that complacency can be very dangerous. Most people fail not when they're taking risks, but when they sit back and relax. You'll be blinded to this if you believe you've already made it. While you're sitting in your place of power, enjoying the view, someone below you is learning from you. Someone, who has been motivated and inspired by you is ready to switch up the structure. We can't be blinded by our own egos. We can't create that kind of bubble for ourselves. Fortunately, there's always a room with someone smarter in it. It's easy to stick to what we know. Somehow, we find comfort in surrounding ourselves with people who seem further behind than us. But what does this achieve? How does that challenge us? This perspective is like hanging out with grade school students, and boasting when we beat them. We may have outsmarted them; but what vision of ourselves have we created in them?

I am never the smartest person in the room. I intentionally learn from college students, colleagues, my wife, my children, and anyone in a room with me. This is not about me being big and you being little; it's about me becoming the best that I can be.

The only way I will become my best is if I continue to learn, grow, and strive for better. Most of our egos are inflated daily because underneath, we are insecure and worried someone may find out who we really are. We become frightened about being average—and we should be, if we don't have the right individuals around us! However, when you have smarter people in the room with you, along with those who are learning from you, it's a win-win situation!

We must always have the desire to learn, grow, and strive. That may not mean a better score, job, or social standing; it simply means a better version of me. Somewhere out there are rooms in which I must feel small and inadequate in order to be challenged and grow myself. All I have to do is open the door and enter. In my transition, there is someone willing to expand me, teach me, and help me develop into my destiny!

For Thought:

1. In what areas of your life are you tired of being average?

2. Who is bringing you down that you might need to remove from your life?

3. What kind of people do you need surrounding you? Where will you find these people?

chapter 4

A SHIFT IS COMING

AVE YOU EVER TRIED to make a puzzle piece fit in the wrong place? Have you ever tried to put a square peg in a round hole? How many pairs of jeans do you try on before you find the perfect fit? This was my dilemma in finding the right person to take over Living Faith Tabernacle as my successor. Many people do not understand the business side of ministry. However, you can't have a ministry without this aspect. This book is not designed for pastors and ministers only; it is my desire to lead those in corporate and ministry positions through transition in a healthy manner. I want to empower you so that you will not die full, but empty, having given everything you have to fulfill your destiny on earth.

For nearly 27 years, I woke up as the senior pastor and founder of my local congregation. I rolled out of bed with a full schedule and new challenges to face in my growing church in Forest Park, Georgia. I loved my job, my life, and even the challenges that it brought each day, because every day was different. I can honestly say that I loved my job at least 97 percent of the time. I was fortunate to see our congregation grow from a small handful of followers. We went through seven different building increases and ended up with a sanctuary that seats 1,100. We have multiple services each week. We saw success in every aspect of our ministry, which was especially exciting for a small-town boy from South Charleston, Ohio.

This book has been designed to break every thought pattern that has been taught concerning transition. Often, we are taught to ride a horse until he won't go any further. But this book will give you a new view of how to pass the torch. You do not have to die behind the pulpit of a fading church, or leave a company only after it goes belly-up. You do not have to leave tired, burned out, or frustrated. You can leave a healthy organization and be in a healthy place yourself. Our callings often require us to change altitude, and we must be comfortable with that. In my younger days, this was called *faith* and *trust*. Somehow, we tend to lose a piece of that vital product that has been entrusted to us.

We are taught that pastors—especially founding pastors—are given a life sentence to our churches. CEOs and entrepreneurs can also buy the notion that they can never move on from their current venture. Please do not misunderstand: I loved my job and the people I worked with—I had great relationships with them. I worked with great people. However, at about the 25-year mark, I knew my calling was shifting. I had no idea what was being planned for my life, and it seemed as if the Greater Power wouldn't reveal it to me all at once. This would be a journey in which I would have to take baby steps, listening closely.

How do you stop doing what you love when it's all you have ever known? Since I was 24, I had eaten, drunk, talked, walked, and lived Living Faith Tabernacle. How do you move forward when no one is showing you what to do? The only thing you can do is trust that you are being led to do greater things. If I had been disgruntled or angry with my parishioners, then I would understand the need for transition. But that was not my situation. I was not too old to be effective, and no one was pushing me out. It was simply the end of one season and the beginning of the next. Sometimes your ending is really your new beginning. I had trusted this process for years; but now I was truly out of my element.

I had become familiar with the place I was in, and its success. I had gotten myself into a routine, and it had become a rut. Why? Because the church was outgrowing me, and I was outgrowing the church at the same time. We both had a new calling. Fortunately, my wife and I had never lived beyond our means. If we couldn't pay for it, we didn't need it or get it. We struggled month to month for 30 years to pay for what we believe we deserve. Many times, people try to prove a point—that God can bless us—in a foolish way, and end up getting their home repossessed. How does that portray God? God takes care of the sparrows and the lilies, and He will take care of us. We can be so concerned about what others think we should have; however, at the end of the day, it's my responsibility to make sure I pay to keep what I own.

Many individuals who have seen my transition ask me, "How can you afford to walk away?" My answer is that I lived within my means. I am trusting that other, greater doors will be opened because of faith and obedience. Unfortunately, many churches in America are paying the price for keeping their pastors poor. Pastors try to prove they're living in prosperity, but in reality, they and their churches are suffering. I am a firm believer that churches and corporations must take care of their pastors and CEOs; and pastors and CEOs must do right with their spending habits.

My biggest challenge was finding the right fit. I have an entire chapter dedicated to this topic later. My goal wasn't to find a successor I could manipulate and control; it was to find a successor I could trust and follow. His vision would not be my vision, and that's all right. I have never been afraid of great ideas that were different.

Many predecessors want to keep successors under their thumbs. But it's important to realize that, in corporations and churches, there will be only one *true* head. Anything with more than one head is a monster. We need boards; we need visionaries; but we must have a leader with a clear direction. I had the responsibility of leading my church for 27 years; now the mantle needed to be passed, so the light could stay lit and bright for the journey. I knew it would take a unique person to lead the Tabernacle.

"Transitions in life can offer opportunities for discovery." —Robbie Shell

---

My journey began when, in my spirit, I was given a specific date nearly two years before the transition: December 31, 2016. I thought two years would be plenty of time. I could train, develop, watch, and critique my successor into the position. The search began for the right fit. I thought it would be a no-brainer. Boy, was I wrong! It's not easy privately searching out your successor. If I had posted the position, many would have come to try out to lead such a thriving ministry. But that's not what I did. I was instructed by my Greater Power to "privately seek out my chosen one, and when you find them, you will know." I was up for the challenge. It's similar to the story of Samuel seeking out Israel's king in 1 Samuel 16. Each time Samuel thought he'd found the right man, God told him, "This is not the one." Why didn't God simply show him the next king? Because the journey is what strengthens and gives power. In 1 Samuel 16, the story is shared:

The Lord said to Samuel, "How long will you mourn for Saul, since I have rejected him as king over Israel? Fill your horn with oil and be on your way; I am sending you to Jesse of Bethlehem. I have chosen one of his sons to be king."

But Samuel said, "How can I go? If Saul hears about it, he will kill me."

The Lord said, "Take a heifer with you and say, 'I have come to sacrifice to the Lord.' Invite Jesse to the sacrifice, and I will show you what to do. You are to anoint for me the one I indicate."

Samuel did what the Lord said. When he arrived at Bethlehem, the elders of the town trembled when they met him. They asked, "Do you come in peace?"

Samuel replied, "Yes, in peace; I have come to sacrifice to the Lord. Consecrate yourselves and come to the sacrifice with me." Then he consecrated Jesse and his sons and invited them to the sacrifice.

When they arrived, Samuel saw Eliab and thought, "Surely the Lord's anointed stands here before the Lord."

But the Lord said to Samuel, "Do not consider his appearance or his height, for I have rejected him. The Lord does not look at the things people look at. People look at the outward appearance, but the Lord looks at the heart."

Then Jesse called Abinadab and had him pass in front of Samuel. But Samuel said, "The Lord has not chosen this one either." Jesse then had Shammah pass by, but Samuel said, "Nor has the Lord chosen this one." Jesse had seven of his sons pass before Samuel, but Samuel said to him, "The Lord has not chosen these." So he asked Jesse, "Are these all the sons you have?"

"There is still the youngest," Jesse answered. "He is tending the sheep."

Samuel said, "Send for him; we will not sit down until he arrives."

So he sent for him and had him brought in. He was glowing with health and had a fine appearance and handsome features.

Then the Lord said, "Rise and anoint him; this is the one."

So Samuel took the horn of oil and anointed him
in the presence of his brothers, and from that day on
the Spirit of the Lord came powerfully upon David.
Samuel then went to Ramah. (NIV)

Now God had released me for the search and given me two years to develop His chosen one. Simple, right? Not at all. God would challenge my faith and leadership, taking me through betrayal and trust before this man was revealed. I began secretly having lunches, bringing speakers in, and attending services, hunting for the person God wanted. It would not come easily. Lunch guests stood me up; there were no-shows; integrity issues kept me away from so many about whom I'd thought, "This is the one." When someone would no-show or cancel, it would be declared to me, "That's not the one." If they had known ahead of time what I was doing, most would have shown up on time, in a suit and tie, and offered to buy me lunch. But that wasn't the instruction I received. My instructions were to lie low and watch, and I would know. *Come on, God, just tell me,* I thought; but it was the search that would develop me for the next phase of my life. We often say, "If I knew then what I know now..." However, it's the push that makes us strong.

I once heard a story about a man and a rock. The man was hired to press against a boulder in front of a man's house. Day in and day out, the man would come to do the same job. He would put all of his weight into pushing this large rock. After a few weeks, the man became discouraged and quit. His employer asked him why he was quitting. The young man said, "For weeks I have been pushing on this huge rock and I have not moved it a centimeter." The landlord looked at him and said, "But you have done a fine job. You have done what I asked. I did not ask you to move the rock—only to push against it. Now look at you. Your arms are stronger; your legs have more strength and you have become a powerful man. Now you are ready to work on the farm because your muscles have been developed." We must remember, God is looking for obedience. He can move the rock, or anything else He desires, at any time. He is seeking those who are willing to simply obey Him.

More than a year went by, and I still hadn't found the right person. I had a slipper and no foot to fit it! Cinderella was going to turn up in a pumpkin instead of her carriage! My successor was nowhere to be found! Then on a cold February night, at a late hour, I shot out of bed. My wife, Kathy, asked, "Honey, what is it?" I explained to her that I was hearing December 31 would be the transition day. Now, I was worried. Only ten months to the deadline, and no successor in sight! Had I heard God correctly? Was he going to transition me to heaven instead? I asked, "God, where are you? What am I to do?

Time is closing in on me!" God continued to quicken my spirit to find the missing piece.

Life is a puzzle. Every piece has a place, but every piece may not go into the place you think is right. If you look at the front of the puzzle box, you see the entire picture. It takes work, strategy, and time to complete it. Once you put one piece in the wrong place, it throws the entire puzzle out of balance.

Life is also like a car. A car has four tires. It takes only one tire to get the whole car out of alignment. In other words, if you're 25 percent out of alignment, your entire life can be thrown out of balance. Seventy-five percent of your tires can be working, but that remaining 25 percent will wear you out. If not fixed, one tire can mess up the front end suspension of the car and, eventually, the mechanical system. A simple fix, when ignored, has the potential of ruining the entire vehicle.

Everyone knows when you are out of alignment—in church, your organization, your company, your life, or your family. The kids, as they bounce in the backseat, know it; the wife, as she rides along, knows the car is out of balance. We think people don't know, but everyone sees who is out of alignment! The Bible tells us in Galatians 5:9, "A little yeast works through the whole batch of dough" (NIV).

It was essential for Living Faith to have the senior pastor puzzle piece in its proper place. I loved these people and this church. Twenty-seven years of my life had been put into building it. I wanted it to succeed and be better. A wise person once told me that the success of a leader is not revealed until he has been gone for a year. If his establishment survives and grows, he was a great leader; if it fails in the first year without him, it was all hype, and leadership was never imparted to the people. I cherish time. I cannot make more time, so I respect it. I do not want to look back and regret spending 27 years on something that ultimately fails.

People came and went; still, I had no prospects in mind. I didn't think I had enough time left to develop someone. Had I missed my sign? Was the Big Man Upstairs mad at me? Was my life ending? No answers came—only questions. Finally, in July, the time came to share my heart with the executive board. My time was wrapping up, and my mission was almost complete. They assumed I was tired and discouraged, but I was neither. I was excited, but had no one to present to them as my successor. The same questions kept swirling in my mind: *Where is this piece to this puzzle? Am I simply being tested for my willingness? I'm only five months away; what am I to do?* I finally concluded that I must have misunderstood the calling to find a successor. I relaxed. After all, I figured, everyone knows you can't always be right. *This is the one I missed,* I thought. *A major one, but I missed it.*

One of the first people I had considered was Jeremy Tuck in Newnan, Georgia. We'd met and discovered it wasn't a fit for either of us. Now, at the end of August, God asked, "Have you considered my servant Jeremy?" Laughing aloud, I answered, "God, yes! He was my first choice, but he didn't fit." Out of nowhere, God showed me the puzzle. I said it again: "But God, it isn't a fit." God replied, "It wasn't a fit then, but try the piece now." I answered, "God, we've already parted from the idea. It didn't work." God then told me that neither Jeremy nor I had been ready at that time. He had needed to take us both on a journey to identify what he showed us months ago. It couldn't be based on Jeremy's will, and it couldn't be based on mine. It had to be God's will and God's timing.

Reluctantly, I sent a text to Jeremy: "Hey, just thinking about you today and praying for you. I am not sure that you are not who I have been looking for ... your thoughts?" Jeremy immediately reached out to me, expressing his fears at the thought. He had been successful in growing a rural church and in breaking unbelievable barriers.

God showed me that, when you are out of your element, you cease to exist. There are certain things that cannot live out of their element. When you're away from God, you are out of your element. In fact, when you're lacking, you aren't doing what you were created to do.

You were created in the image of God, and God is not a God of lack! When we're bogged down with life, we've moved to a dimension God never intended. He created us to be like Him and live a life of *peace*. Remember 2 Corinthians 12:10, which tells us that when we are weak, He makes us strong? Joel 3:10 also says, "Let the weak say, I am strong!" (KJV).

How do we know if we're out of our element? When things are taken out of their element, they cease to exist. For example, when a star falls, it ceases to exist. Why? Because it was created to exist in the sky. It can't survive elsewhere. If you take a fish out of water, it dies. Why? Because you have removed it from its element. When you pull a plant out of the ground, it dies. Our natural element is to have communion with God and to worship Him. We were created to worship God! When something is taken out of its natural habitat, it ceases to exist!

Jeremy was out of his element in his own church, and I was out of mine. He was the piece that was missing from the puzzle for Living Faith. I knew then that he was the one. He was my successor; but it was the end of September before we figured this out. How was God going to pull this off? Now that I'd begun this journey, there was no turning back. I thought, *What do I do next?*

For Thought:

1. What puzzle piece have you tried to force into the wrong place?

2. What have you released from your life that you once thought was permanent?

3. Is there anything currently out of alignment in your life? What can you do to regain balance in this area?

chapter 5

FINDING THE RIGHT FIT

INDING THE RIGHT FIT is never easy. It takes, time, persistence, dedication, and patience. This is true in many facets of life. If a young woman finds her knight in shining armor, but he is not drawn to her and not willing to commit, it is not a perfect fit. I've had session after session with young couples in love, in which the woman says, "I know he's not in church now, but he will come when we get married!" This philosophy always amazes me. My response is, "Are you willing to stay in the relationship if he doesn't come to church?" Of course, the answer is always the same, and typically, the result is eventually the same as well. It's unfortunate, but all too real.

Often, when we become desperate, we become willing to settle for something less than God's perfect plan for our lives. We suffer for long periods of time—often it's actually a lifetime of suffering, because we didn't wait for the perfect fit. Most times, by not waiting, we interfere with the outcome and hamper our destiny. I've heard many people talk about their ex-spouses by saying, "If only I had waited, how different life would be!"

As founder of Living Faith, I had only one shot at getting this right. I would turn my legacy over to a man who would either be my successor or my traitor! As in marriage, I only had one shot. I've been married to my beautiful wife, Kathy, for 35 years. I know I found my perfect fit. There are no do-overs. I had to get that decision right, just as I had to get the correct successor in position. I must admit, Jeremy and I have a unique story because most predecessors do not want their successors to outshine them. However, in Scripture we see that Elisha outshines Elijah. Elijah, the older of the two, tests Elisha on his faithfulness. In 2 Kings 2, Elijah tells Elisha to stay where he is:

*When the L*ORD *was about to take Elijah up to heaven in a whirlwind, Elijah and Elisha were on* *their way from Gilgal. Elijah said to Elisha, "Stay here; the LORD has sent me to Bethel."*

But Elisha said, "As surely as the LORD lives and as you live, I will not leave you." So they went down to Bethel. The company of the prophets at Bethel came out to Elisha and asked, "Do you know that the LORD is going to take your master from you today?" "Yes, I know," Elisha replied, "so be quiet." Then Elijah said to him, "Stay here, Elisha; the LORD has sent me to Jericho." And he replied, "As surely as the LORD lives and as you live, I will not leave you." So they went to Jericho. The company of the prophets at Jericho went up to Elisha and asked him, "Do you know that the LORD is going to take your master from you today?" "Yes, I know," he replied, "so be quiet." Then Elijah said to him, "Stay here; the LORD has sent me to the Jordan." And he replied, "As surely as the LORD lives and as you live, I will not leave you." So the two of them walked on. Fifty men from the company of the prophets went and stood at a distance, facing the place where Elijah and Elisha had stopped at the Jordan. Elijah took his cloak, rolled it up and struck the water with it. The water divided to the right and to the left, and the two of them crossed over on dry ground. When they had crossed, Elijah said to Elisha, "Tell me, what can I do for you before I am taken from you?" "Let me inherit a double portion of your spirit," Elisha replied. "You have asked a difficult thing," Elijah said, "yet if you see me when I am taken from you, it will be yours—otherwise, it will not." As they were walking along and talking together, suddenly a chariot of fire and horses of fire appeared and separated the two of them, and Elijah went up to heaven in a whirlwind. Elisha saw this and cried out, "My father! My father! The chariots and horsemen of Israel!" And Elisha saw him no more. Then he took hold of his garment and tore it in two. Elisha then picked up Elijah's cloak that had fallen from him and went back and stood on the bank of the Jordan. He took the cloak that had fallen from Elijah and struck the water with it. "Where now is the LORD, the God of Elijah?" he asked. When he struck the water, it divided to the right and to the left, and he crossed over.

In the same way that Elisha had a double portion of Elijah's anointing, I knew that Jeremy would outshine me in his role as my successor. It is God's will for the kingdom.

Another Bible story comes to mind—the one in which Naomi tested Ruth by telling her to go back to her homeland. Ruth refused, and would not go back.

Why? Because she was committed, and this commitment advanced them into a great realm. Let's look at Ruth chapter 1:

When Naomi heard in Moab that the LORD had come to the aid of his people by providing food for them, she and her daughters-in-law prepared to return home from there. With her two daughters-in-law she left the place where she had been living and set out on the road that would take them back to the land of Judah.

Then Naomi said to her two daughters-in-law, "Go back, each of you, to your mother's home. May the LORD show you kindness, as you have shown kindness to your dead husbands and to me. May the LORD grant that each of you will find rest in the home of another husband."

Then she kissed them goodbye and they wept aloud and said to her, "We will go back with you to your people."

But Naomi said, "Return home, my daughters. Why would you come with me? Am I going to have any more sons, who could become your husbands? Return home, my daughters; I am too old to have another husband. Even if I thought there was still hope for me—even if I had a husband tonight and then gave birth to sons—would you wait until they grew up? Would you remain unmarried for them? No, my daughters. It is more bitter for me than for you, because the LORD's hand has turned against me!"

At this they wept aloud again. Then Orpah kissed her mother-in-law goodbye, but Ruth clung to her.

"Look," said Naomi, "your sister-in-law is going back to her people and her gods. Go back with her."

But Ruth replied, "Don't urge me to leave you or to turn back from you. Where you go I will go, and where you stay I will stay. Your people will be my people and your God my God. Where you die I will die, and there I will be buried. May the LORD deal with me, be it ever so severely, if even death separates you and me." When Naomi realized that Ruth was determined to go with her, she stopped urging her.

Jeremy has proved to be an amazing successor. He has proven himself to be faithful, not only to God and the church, but also to me! I know that many are reading this, saying, "This is what I desire; but how can I experience it?" The answer is quite simple! Prayer, persistence, and patience. I must have secretly interviewed 140 men and women to be my successor, but none seemed to be the perfect fit. It got disheartening, discouraging, and frustrating, but I knew that my pastorate was coming to an end.

Many people ask me, "How did you know it was time to choose a successor?" That is quite simple as well: When you lose your passion and stop having the dreams you used to have every night, it's time to go. Don't get me wrong: I loved what I did; I loved the people, and I loved the Lord most of all. God simply changed my vision. My ministry has moved to new levels I could never have imagined, and I am dreaming again! Because we transitioned Living Faith to a man who had the *next* dream, both of us were able to further fulfill our purposes in life!

"Change is situational. Transition, on the other hand, is psychological."
—William Bridges

The perfect fit—how does it feel? Have you ever had a suit tailor-fitted to your body? It's a totally different feeling than buying off the rack. Many men can fit into the same 42 R suit; but when the suit is tailor-made, it hugs the body and flows with perfection! Others may try it on, but it will never fit or feel the way it does on the one for whom it was designed. Many will say, "Who can afford that? It costs ten times what off-the-rack suits cost!" This is the wrong mindset! Let me ask you a question: What does it cost you when you pick the wrong fit in marriage? What does it cost when you pick the wrong job? What does it cost when you invest in the wrong stocks? The list could go on. It pays more, in the long run, to find the perfect fit.

Several months ago, I spent time reconstructing my cabin in the mountains. I spent one of my days there going up and down the ladder in the wrong shoes. Today, as a result of that choice, I still have to wisely choose shoes that won't make my feet ache after just a few minutes. I have considered surgery, shots, and anything else that will relieve the pain. I've had to stop doing cardio workouts, going on long walks, taking the stairs, and things that I took for granted so many times. If only I'd had the perfect-fitting shoes on that particular day. What would they have cost? A hundred dollars? Two hundred? Five hundred? I wouldn't even care today! I've lost well over $500 in pain. I've lost well over $500 in missed opportunities, all because of the wrong fit.

As you can see, having the right fit means everything. It decreases your pain, ups your game, and, at the end of the day, gives you peace. There is nothing worse than waking up one day and realizing you've made a decision that will alter the rest of your life in a negative way. You have to get it right; and when you do, you have to move quickly. Having the right fit feels amazing!

For Thought:

1. Think about a specific area in your life that's in transition. What would be the perfect fit for you?

2. How much are you willing to invest to reach your life goal?

3. Think of an experience in which you were not willing to pay the price for the perfect fit. What was the outcome? In retrospect, would you choose differently?

chapter 6

MY SUCCESSOR'S POINT OF VIEW

by Jeremy Tuck

I HAD BEEN THE PASTOR of Oak Grove Baptist Church for seven years when Dr. Chris Bowen approached me to take the Living Faith Tabernacle position.

My journey at Oak Grove had been remarkable. At the start of the church, we'd had 15 members and no money. You would not have been able to find the church on a GPS. I had so many questions: "Can I grow this? Can I turn this around? God, did you really call me to this?" To be completely honest, I had many sleepless nights wondering if I'd heard God correctly. One year passed, and the church didn't grow. I remained consistent and trusted God. In year two, the church began to grow astronomically. Each Sunday, the congregation would get larger and larger. After four years, we were packing the 300-seat auditorium, which we outgrew in the fifth year. Our growth became so massive that we purchased 6.7 acres of land and made plans to build a brand new sanctuary. I was six years in, and the church was still growing. There were many days that I said to myself, "I'm going to retire here; I'm going to raise my kids here."

Then, Dr. Chris Bowen came to me and said, "I think you are my successor." Of course, the question in the back of mind was, "A successor to what?" Dr. Bowen went on to say that it was time for him to transition from Living Faith Tabernacle, and that I was to be his successor. My initial response was, "I think you have the wrong guy." I began to tell him about all the things we were doing at the church. He looked at me and said, "All those things are great! But I know that you are my successor."

After concluding lunch with him that day, I must admit that I was puzzled by the invitation. There were so many unanswered questions. I thought, "Why would he want to give his church to someone like me? What do I have to offer a church of that size and magnitude? Also, in case you haven't noticed, I am a black man and you're a white man. What if I take this church and ruin it? What if I get there, and the people don't receive me?" After we met that day, the only thing I could think was, "There's no way I'm leaving my church; I have no reason." The church was vibrant and growing. There was no possible way that God was in this offer. I began to ask Him, "Why didn't you send this opportunity during my first year with my church?" After all, it would have been easy to say "yes" if Dr. Bowen had offered me the position during my first pastoral year.

"Action is the key to transition."
—Awakening the Greatness Within

I was approaching my seventh year as the pastor of Oak Grove Baptist Church, and had finally made up my mind that I was going to stay. I convinced myself that it was God's will for me to remain where I was. However, even though we'd decided I really wasn't a good fit for Living Faith Tabernacle, there was a piece of me that knew I couldn't stay at Oak Grove. It had always been easy for me to accept job promotions; but here I was being given a promotion that just didn't seem right. Many times, I'd preached on 2 Samuel 7:8: ""Now therefore, thus you shall say to My servant David, 'Thus says the LORD of hosts, "I took you from the pasture, from

following the sheep, to be ruler over My people Israel"'''
(NASB). Many times, pastors preach something that we
ourselves don't even believe.

Oak Grove was in a great place, but my vision had begun to outgrow the church. We paid off the acreage.
Unfortunately, the building plans had been halted by
the board. They wanted to wait at least four to five years
before starting the project. I explained to them that
time waits for no one, and that we must strike while the
iron is hot. During this process, Dr. Bowen resurfaced
with the message, "I know that you are my successor."
After prayer and careful consideration, I made one of
the hardest decisions I've ever had to make in my life: to
leave Oak Grove, the church I had grown from 15 people
to almost 400.

I actually thought leaving was going to be easier; but
on the day I made the announcement, it seemed more
like a funeral. I burst into tears, weeping as if I had lost
it all. Fear began to overtake me. People were crying
all over the sanctuary, and the fact that there was utter
silence made the situation even more awkward. After
about 15 minutes of tears, people suddenly began to
stand and clap, saying things like, "You deserve this,"
"We understand," "This is your moment," and, "You
have done your job here, and you have done it well!" It
was this moment that gave me complete assurance I had
made the right decision.

On December 31, 2016, I officially became the pastor of Living Faith Tabernacle in Forest Park, Georgia. I was excited but also haunted by fear. Feelings of inadequacy, and the question of whether I had what it took to pastor an urban church, gripped me. I was extremely successful at pastoring a rural church, but this felt out of my league. I was definitely out of my comfort zone. Still, I knew, along with Dr. Bowen, that I was the right fit!

For Thought:

1. What is your current succession plan?

2. What would hold you back from reaching your destiny?

3. Name a goal you've already reached that, at one time, you felt was unobtainable?

chapter 7

THE CHALLENGES

I KNEW WITHOUT A SHADOW of doubt that Jeremy Tuck was the pastor to take Living Faith to new levels. I was excited about the future for him, his family, the church, and for myself! There was just one slight little detail—one issue—that challenged me: What was I going to do now?

I'd spent all my time and energy trying to make sure I dotted every "i" and crossed every "t"—to ensure all would be in place for Jeremy and the church to provide a smooth and healthy transition. I honestly hadn't paused long enough to think about what I would do once I left that awesome place and the people who had become my life for the past 27 years! I knew I was in the center of God's will by passing the torch to my successor; however,

I had no direction from Him about where He'd take me from there.

In all my years as pastor, one thing that remained constant about me was a passion for change. I've always loved to keep things moving. I wanted to make sure Living Faith avoided falling into the common rut of making each and every service looks the same. No one could ever accuse me of being predictable. Even my wife would tease me, saying she would never sit down at home without checking behind her to make sure the chair was still there—I was constantly rearranging the furniture! There were times I'd undergo building projects at the church, not out of necessity, but simply because I knew staying still could easily lead to complacency: the place that destroys so many churches. In ministry, one of our biggest threats is becoming comfortable with where we are. We should always be growing! I had a reputation as being the "Energizer Bunny." I'm always on the go, never slowing down. I like to keep things moving and people guessing about what will come next!

Now, I suddenly found myself having to come to a screeching halt. I'd done all the right things: found the perfect leader for the church, ensured that the transition was as smooth as possible for the staff and congregation, prepared myself for the emotions that would come for everyone with the passing of the mantle. The time had come for me to face the fact that I was unemployed, with no new job in place. Yes, I knew my time of pastoring was done. The door had shut, and my 27 years as pastor of Living Faith Tabernacle would be a part of my history, not my current description. *Lord,* I thought, *where do we go from here?*

In Genesis Chapter 12, we read the story of Abram. God speaks to him about his future, commanding him, "Leave your country and your people. Leave your father's family and go to the country that I will show you." How many of us would pack our belongings and our families with only those vague instructions as a guide? Basically, all Abram had to work with was, "Go." He didn't get the script any more fully than that.

In today's world, we don't want to do anything without getting play-by-play instructions. Instead, we put a fleece (or two, or three) before the Lord, making ridiculous bargains with Him: "Lord, if this is really you, make the lights flicker three times," or, "Lord, if you really want me to go to church tomorrow morning, let my alarm go off without me even setting it." It's a wonder God doesn't just zap us for some of the crazy things we ask of Him.

Here I was, in a situation where God was sending me away from all that was familiar. This transition was truly a test of my faith. It's one thing to leave a job with the promise of a bigger and better one; it's one thing when you have a great salary, an insurance and benefits package, and a 401(k) in place to help prepare for your retirement years. All I had at this point was the command, "Go." When God gives you the peace that comes with his simple instruction, it's much easier to act on it. Everyone who is in my close circle was convinced that I had an adrenaline rush because God's voice enabled me to be calm and relaxed about my major role change. They were sure that, once I released the role of senior pastor, I would become sad, depressed, and overwhelmed with the sense of loss. They hovered over me, confident I would crumble. But it never happened. I truly experienced the peace that passes all understanding!

I was reminded, even in the midst of this uncertainty, of a sermon I preached years ago. It's titled, "When the What Is Clear, the How Will Appear." I simply had to trust that God, who had made the *what* very clear to me, would in time reveal the *how* to me.

I did know that just because my job at Living Faith was done, it didn't mean I was done. The Lord had opened many doors for me, especially in the previous few years, to speak around the country and internationally. In fact, traveling often was one of the factors that had led me to the decision to turn the church over to a successor. I didn't want to be absent more than present; and I didn't want my obligation to the church to hold me back from the opportunities opening up to me. In most of my pastoral years, I took only Monday-through-Friday vacations,

and wouldn't miss more than one or two Sundays a year. My willingness to trust the congregation with someone else behind the pulpit was a huge sign that I was learning to release my control.

Don't get me wrong: I hadn't lost my love for the people. Living Faith was home. I spent more time in the office and behind the pulpit then I did at home. Some of the members had been there the entire 27 years I had. I'd been a shepherd to the church exactly as many years as I had been a father to my oldest son. My world revolved around the church. Letting go, no matter how confident I was of God's perfect will, was not an easy task.

"Your life is a story of transition. You are always leaving one chapter behind while moving to the next." —Anonymous

---

In Matthew 14, we find the story of the disciples fighting a storm out on the waves. Jesus walked out to them on the water. As soon as they got over their terror, Peter asked Jesus to let him walk out to meet Him. Jesus invited Peter to come! We are so quick to judge Peter for allowing those waves to cause him to sink from fear. But in his defense, at least he was willing to leave the comfort and safety of the boat. That's better than the other disciples did. Just like Peter, it was my turn to step out in

faith, and let go of everything that felt safe and comfortable so that I could have an encounter with Jesus. It was time to launch out!

Although I knew where to leave from, I had no idea where to go. I've always believed, and preached, that if you expect God to bless your life, you need to prepare for that blessing. If you need a financial blessing, but don't even have a bank account, then you aren't preparing for your finances to increase. I was expecting the Lord to bless me with business and speaking engagements. It was up to me to show Him I was serious—not just "naming and claiming," while I did nothing!

I got busy. I found and leased a small, nice office in one of the most popular places in Atlanta: Atlantic Station. This thriving area has office buildings, trendy restaurants, retail stores, health clubs, and theaters. I named my business Five Star Personal and Corporate Development INC, based on the book that I authored, *Beyond 5 Star Quality*. I printed business cards, purchased furniture and decor for the office, and did everything in my power to create a place for the Lord to bless. I was ready!

But, just like the waves that hit Peter when he courageously stepped out of that boat to meet Jesus, a wave of fear tried to strip me of my joy and excitement. What if no one picked up a business card from the many places I'd left them? What if pastors stopped calling me

for speaking engagements? What if businesses were through with my training for Beyond Five Star Quality? What if my opportunities to travel overseas had ended with my title of "pastor"? Those thoughts came to mind just like unexpected storms! But within a few moments, it was as if the Lord spoke to every negative thought that crossed my mind, "Peace, be still!"

As a pastor, leader, or business owner, your faith will be tested. Sometimes, the Lord gives you the *what* and *how* at the same time. At other times, He simply says, "Go." Just like a father does with his children, God may or may not explain why He does things. We simply have to obey, with no questions asked.

When my sons were little, I could stand them on top of the refrigerator and tell them to jump. They would get excited, smile, and jump with no hesitation at all. As they started to get older, they hesitated a bit, and I had to convince them that I would catch them. They eventually reached the size and age that they no longer trusted in me to catch them! This is how we are in our walk with the Lord. When we first receive the free gift of salvation, our faith is big! We trust Him with everything! We are excited and obey everything He asks of us. Why is it that, after a little time, we forget that He is our Father—that He is more than capable of catching us in our time of need? I believe this is why the Scripture tells us in Matthew 18:3, "Unless you change and become like little children, you will never enter the kingdom of heaven." It's just like the old song says: "Trust and obey; for there's no other way to be happy in Jesus, but to trust and obey!"

I believe with all of my heart that, if I'd simply left Living Faith, went home to my wife and sat down on the couch with satisfaction, I would be in line for unemployment to this day! I had to get busy preparing for the next chapter of my life.

God's Word tells us, in Hebrews 11:6, that without faith, it is impossible to please Him, but that He rewards those who diligently seek Him. The definition of diligence is "constant effort to accomplish something" or "persistent pursuit of something." You will never advance in your goals by sitting on your La-Z-Boy patiently waiting for an instructional letter from God to appear in your mailbox. It's time to get busy. God may have given you the *what* and the *go*, but not the *how*. He'll give you more when you prove you can be trusted with it. He wants to see what you're willing to do with what he's given you so far. Once you obey with the little commands, He will begin to give you details of how to make the dream happen!

For Thought:

1. Now that you've read the first half of this book, what would you say your greatest challenges are?

2. How long have you been stuck? In what area(s) are you currently stuck?

3. What is the first step you need to take to get out of your comfort zone?

chapter 8

METAMORPHOSIS

ETAMORPHOSIS IS THE PROCESS of transformation from an immature form to an adult form. If someone or something has gone through metamorphosis, they have been changed into a completely different thing, either naturally or supernaturally. When we think of metamorphosis, we tend to refer to the stages of a caterpillar turning into a butterfly, or a tadpole transforming into a frog. Any time metamorphosis takes place, it's a remarkable occurrence.

I preached a sermon many years ago on this subject. In giving examples of Biblical people who went through transformations, I shared the story in 1 Samuel 10:6, in which Samuel anointed Saul. Samuel says, "The Spirit of the Lord will come powerfully upon you, and you will prophesy with them; *and you will be changed into a different person*" (emphasis mine, NIV). When we read on to verse 9, it says, "As Saul turned to leave Samuel, God changed Saul's heart, and all these signs were fulfilled that day." Saul not only became a new man spiritually; he also became king of a nation!

In Genesis 17:5-8, we read the story of the Lord changing Abram's name to Abraham. He becomes the father of Isaac at the ripe old age of 100, and God doesn't stop there. Abraham becomes the father of many nations. Here's someone who truly experienced metamorphosis in his life!

In the New Testament, we have the example of another man named Saul. His story starts off as that of an enemy of the church. In fact, Saul makes it his life's work to destroy the teachings of Jesus. He is passionate about this purpose. In Acts 9, we read of the metamorphosis that changed not only his name, but his entire life! On the road to Damascus, Saul is blinded by a light and hears a voice speak plainly to him: "Saul, Saul, why do you persecute me?" From that moment, everything in his life changes. Saul, now Paul, becomes one of the most influential followers of Christ who ever lived.

Complacency with where we are—in our careers, marriages, education, spiritual lives, physical well-being, and life in general—is one of the most dangerous things we can allow in our lives. When we stop changing, we start dying. I've been around pastors for well over 30 years; I've heard several say, "If this ship sinks, I'll just go down with it!" That's not a statement of commitment or dedication—that's stubbornness! When you'd rather your ship sink with you at the helm than sail majestically under someone else's hand, that says a lot about you.

We all need to experience a metamorphosis. Change is not a crime, a sin, or a reason for shame. It's a beautiful experience. Change isn't painless or carefree. Sometimes, it's filled with hurt and tears. But transformation is the best thing that could ever happen to us!

In my personal metamorphosis, I arrived at a comfortable place in my pastorate: I loved my church, the people, and the joy of working as a minister each day. I never experienced the burnout so many pastors endure. After 26 and a half years, I felt as if I could remain pastor of Living Faith until the Lord called me home. That was my first indication it was time for change! The church was still growing and healthy, but God was performing a metamorphosis in me personally. It was as if He was saying to me, "Son, I have something totally different I want to turn you into." It was time for change—for both Living Faith and myself.

A tadpole may think he's just fine. He can swim all day, hanging out with others who are just like him. He's never experienced life outside the water. But when metamorphosis starts to take place, he becomes uncomfortable. Suddenly, he is no longer bound to the water. He can now leap on dry land and go beyond all his former limits. A caterpillar could be perfectly content with crawling around, climbing up trees, and munching on leaves; but when it goes through metamorphosis, it experiences a beautiful transformation and is then able to fly!

Do you find yourself stuck? Have you been in the same place for so long that you can't remember anything different? Even though you may be comfortable, don't you think it's time to experience a beautiful transformation? You can change your habits, your negative thinking, or your attitude and have a life more incredible than you've ever imagined. However, it will require willingness to go through the process. Submit yourself to the One who brings about beautiful, incredible change. You will find true happiness and fulfillment beyond your dreams!

We can all name people—whether celebrities, acquaintances, or family members—who have experienced metamorphosis. Maybe they were once poor, and now are in a place of financial freedom. Maybe they went through mental or physical abuse that caused them to reach a point of desperation. Miraculously, they've not only found the strength to come out of their situation, but healing and the ability to help others, as well! Maybe a loved one was on drugs or alcohol, and everyone gave up hope of ever seeing change in their addiction. Now, they are not only clean and sober, but are helping others find hope of overcoming their bondages!

No matter what the situation, these life-changing transformations took place because these people made the decision to do whatever it took. They became willing to endure the pain of the process for the sake of the desired change. Metamorphosis isn't an easy fix. It takes time. It takes a lot of uncomfortable stretching. It's often dark and lonely. It may require giving up people who are holding you back from growth. Transformation isn't easy, but it's sure worth it!

Any transition serious enough to alter your definition of self will require not just small adjustments in your way of living and thinking but a full-on metamorphosis."
—Martha Beck

Let's take a look at a great example of this process. Probably the greatest example of persistence, transformation, and transition is that of our sixteenth president, Abraham Lincoln. If you want to learn about someone who didn't quit, you don't have to look any further. President Lincoln was born into poverty and faced obstacles and defeat throughout his life. He lost eight elections, failed twice in business, and suffered a nervous breakdown. He could have quit on many occasions—but he didn't. Because he didn't quit, he became one of the greatest presidents in the history of our country.

Lincoln was determined and refused to give up. Here are the steps of Lincoln's road to the White House:

- 1816—He was forced out of his home, along with his family. He worked to support them.
- 1818—He lost his mother.
- 1831—He failed in business.
- 1832—He ran for state legislature—and lost.
- 1832—He lost his job. Lincoln wanted to go to law school, but couldn't get in.
- 1833—He borrowed money from a friend to begin a business. By the end of the year, he was bankrupt. He spent the next 17 years of his life paying off this debt.
- 1834—He ran for state legislature again, and won.
- 1835—He was engaged to be married, but his sweetheart died.
- 1836—He had a total nervous breakdown and was in bed for six months.
- 1838—He sought to become speaker of the state legislature, but was defeated.
- 1840—He sought to become elector, and was defeated.
- 1843—He ran for Congress, and lost.

- 1846—He ran for Congress again, and won. He went to Washington and performed well.
- 1848—He ran for re-election to Congress, but lost.
- 1849—He sought the job of land officer in his home state, but was rejected.
- 1854—He ran for Senate of the United States, and lost.
- 1856—He sought the Vice-Presidential nomination at his party's national convention, and got fewer than 100 votes.
- 1858—He ran for U.S. Senate again, and lost.
- 1860—He was elected President of the United States.

Maybe this story seems removed from our reality. After all, we have only read about Lincoln. What about a legend we are all familiar with, Ms. Oprah Winfrey? *Business Insider* ran a piece titled, "From poverty to a $3 billion fortune—the incredible rags-to-riches story of Oprah Winfrey." The story details how Oprah grew up in a boarding house, living in oppressive poverty. As a child, she was physically and sexually abused. Yet she was a popular high school honor student who earned a full college scholarship.

As a young black woman, Winfrey became a news co-anchor in Baltimore, but she was sexually harassed and fired in less than eight months. She didn't stop trying. Winfrey then got a job hosting a struggling morning talk show, which she transformed into *The Oprah Winfrey Show*. Since then, she has started her own production company, published her own magazine, been nominated for an Academy Award for acting, and started her own cable channel. She owns six homes and a private jet. Chicago has a street named after her.

Now, if these stories doesn't give us a "Vitamin B shot" to never give up, nothing will. Hardship after hardship, struggle after struggle, and defeat after defeat, these people did not stop. So, what is stopping you? It's time to sprout your wings and come out of your cocoon. It is the resistance that makes us strong. Push your way through!

For Thought:

1. What are you transitioning from?

2. What is the cost of your transition?

3. If something were to stop you from bursting out of your cocoon, what would it be?

chapter 9

THE PROMISE, THE PROCESS, AND THE PRODUCT

T'S TRUE THAT there is no progress without process. We like to achieve things easily. However, it's not the easy things that make us strong. When we are stretched by resistance, we see what's really underneath. Can you take the pain? Can you endure? Can you stay the course? If you can, you can become stronger.

When I was getting my doctorate, my university assigned me an advisor. I wish I could say that we saw eye-to-eye and became amazing friends, but that is not the true story. He and I clashed. Everything was a struggle. I finally went to the department head and asked for a new advisor. To my dismay, they would not allow it. In fact, the statement they made to me was, "If you want to get your doctorate from this university, I suggest you find a way to please him." Now I knew my options—I had none! I started re-evaluating my mindset and tried to figure out a way of moving forward in the program. It was transition time.

As I began looking over my journey, I realized I had a great promise. I would get my doctorate. I would finish well and be a better person, professor, and pastor. I love the promise. In fact, we all love the promises life brings us. The promise will make you smile, give you hope, and cause you to do what you've never done.

Then I started thinking about the product. The product, for me, would be holding my thesis in one hand and my doctorate degree in the other. The product would be me walking across the stage as they called, "Dr. Christopher Bowen." We all love the *promise,* and we all love the *product.* However, it is what lies between the two that makes us give up. What is so big that it makes 95 percent of people miss out on their product? The *process.*

We love the *promise,* we adore the *product,* but we despise the *process!* Often, we lose our dream in the midst of the process of transition. We see this happen to a woman in 1 Samuel 4:19-22:

> *Eli's daughter-in-law was pregnant and near the time of delivery. When she heard the news that the ark of God had been captured and that her father-in-law and her husband were dead, she went into labor and gave birth, but was overcome by her labor pains. As she was dying, the women attending her said, "Don't despair; you have given birth to a son." But she did not respond or pay any attention. She named the boy Ichabod, saying, "The glory has departed from Israel"—because of the capture of the ark of God and the deaths of her father-in-law and her husband. She said, "The glory has departed from Israel, for the ark of God has been captured." (NIV)*

This woman lost her life because she allowed her labor pain to take over her. What was meant to be a blessing was the same thing that killed her, because she did not stay the course. She died in the midst of her process. I wonder how many are in the graveyard today because they could not remain during the process of their trials. This inability to endure resulted in heart attacks, high blood pressure, anxiety, migraines... the list goes on. In this story, the woman was trying to see her promise, delivered in the product, but gave up during the process. The promise was dynamic, but the process overwhelmed her. Therefore, she never got to enjoy her product.

We want the promise, but the problem is that we want it *right now!* We want it without going through anything. We live in an instant society, where we stand in front of a microwave telling it to hurry up! We welcome the promise and product, but few endure the process to get to their destinies. We must be able to transition from one point of life to the next without not giving up. Sure, the process is painful. It hurts, and even feels like it will kill us, from time to time. However, if we don't give up, we will win and see the product.

I realize now that my advisor was probably the best professor I had. He stretched me! He didn't make it easy, or give in to my whining about how he was being unfair. He pushed me in the process so that, when I walked across the stage as "Dr. Christopher Bowen," it had more value. I went through excruciating pain to hold my product in my hand. It meant more because it cost me something: sleepless nights, learning where I was unlearned, developing time management skills, and developing people skills. The process made me appreciate the promise, and the product was more than I could ever have imagined.

A few years ago, I was blessed with a brand new Mercedes. It didn't cost me a dime. Someone walked in and gave me the keys to it. I always knew my needs would be met, but a Mercedes was certainly not expected. Let me tell you, it was greatly appreciated. There is a law of sowing and reaping. Everyone knows about it—churches, ministries, corporate America, business owners, and millionaires. It's no secret that if we sow, we will have a harvest day and reap what we have sown. That is the *promise!* The product is simple. I had a new Mercedes! I didn't ask for it, but it is in my garage. However, people don't always see what I had to drive during the process. In 1983, I drove a 1960 Chevy Biscayne to school, and I can tell you that I was not highly sought after because of my vehicle.

"When you are transitioning to a new season of life, the people and situations that are no longer for you will fall away."
—Mandy Hale

Then, I moved up to a 1976 Volare, which was greenish-yellow with the passenger door caved in from a previous wreck. You couldn't hit a pothole in it, or you'd be stranded on the side of the road. From there, it gets worse: 1972 Caprice, 1973 Impala, 1981 Pontiac T1000, 1979 Chevy Monza ... you get the picture. This was the process to my current product. People may look now, but each transition took me from where I was to where

I needed to be. At the end of the day, my product was worth the wait!

You must go through your labor to get to your blessing. Why do we never give birth to our dreams? Why are we afraid to transition from our Ford Taurus to our Mercedes E53 Cabriolet? Because we are afraid to go through the process. We allow the process to kill our dreams because we think it should be pain-free. Some people have been pregnant with dreams for 25 years and still haven't delivered them because they are afraid of the delivery pain.

Two things usually sabotage the process: other people, and the dreamer.

Don't let others discourage you. Don't lose focus and cave in to negativity. If someone tells you that you aren't worthy, or that you aren't strong enough, don't believe them. In the same way, don't sabotage your dream yourself! Don't let fear of failure (or success) take over you. Sometimes, doubt kills the promise. Some people become unfaithful—unfaithfulness can also kill the promise.

Process is a particular course of action intended to achieve a result. You already have the promise. You know the product, and are excited about it. Now, you need to focus on the process. That means embracing transition. Don't let anyone kill your dream during this process, and don't sabotage yourself! Start transitioning within your mind, so that your product can become reality! *You are the only thing stopping you!*

For Thought:

1. What is your promise?

2. What will be the product of your promise?

3. What process do you have to go through to reach your promise?

chapter 10

TIMING IS EVERYTHING

WHEN WE WERE KIDS, we would gather around the swing set at the playground and swing as high as we could. When we reached the highest peak, our stomachs would tie in knots as we dared to jump and land on our feet. Unfortunately, I had to get a lot of bumps, bruises, and cuts before I learned exactly how to make a perfect landing. The key wasn't to see how high you could go, or to sit on the rubber seat the correct way. The key was to know when to let go!

I find that this is the problem with many individuals. Whether it be a senior pastor, a choir director, or the

CEO of a large corporation, the truth remains the same. We never jumped from the swing when we were at our lowest point. We made the plunge at the climax of our swing. When we were soaring higher than we ever had, we let go. Too many times, we raise our company or church to the highest it has ever been, and wait too long to transition, only to watch it plummet to its death.

From my research, I've found the average church will grow for about fifteen years. It then plateaus for three years, and declines back to its size during year five, where it will remain for the rest of its life. Often, this is because we don't know when to let go, and so we hold on too long. In this chapter, I want to uncover some of the reasons CEOs, senior pastors, directors, and those in authority don't let go at the proper times.

First, there is a perceived lack of security. We need both financial security and the security of being needed. Many individuals live beyond their means. They spend all they make instead of laying some aside. Proverbs 21:20 says, "The wise have wealth and luxury, but fools spend whatever they get" (NLT). We want everyone to be impressed with what we have. Many individuals come up to me, knowing I am all about financial freedom, and tell me, "Look at this house God blessed me with!" or "Can you believe it? I got this car with no money down!" My response is always the same: "Let me see your deed or title." That my friend, is prosperity. Prosperity is not about the size of the house you get; it's about the size of the house you pay off. We become insecure because we can't keep up with the Joneses. Let me tell you this: "The Joneses are broke!"

When my wife and I started looking for our successor, we could do it with peace because we'd started financially preparing years in advance. We also realized we needed to downsize our home. Our children had grown up and moved on with their own lives. Even though our house had been paid off for more than ten years, we knew we didn't want to spend money on excessive utility bills, yard maintenance, and upkeep. Therefore, before we picked our successor, we downsized. Did we have to do so? No! But did we want to hold on to a big house simply to prove we could? No! We'd rather live on purpose than impress those who only know us from a distance.

> "Life must be a preparation for the transition to another dimension."
> —Terence McKenna

During this season, individuals asked us, "Is everything all right? We noticed you're downsizing so early in life." Our response remained, "We're living our dream, and a big debt-free house to keep up with isn't part of our plan." People were shocked, because they'd never seen this. When my children were small, I needed a big house. But there came a time to let it go. The Bible tells us that nothing remains the same. Ecclesiastes 3:1 says, "There is a time for everything, and a season for every activity under the heavens."

On the other hand, we all have a need to be needed. Questions of insecurity might sound like this: "What if Pastor Tuck does better than me?" "What if the church grows under him more than I could grow it?" The truth is that I can never be Pastor Jeremy Tuck, and Pastor Jeremy Tuck can never be me. He and I needed to be secure in ourselves to make this transition. He would never have the birthing stories of the church. He will never quite know the struggle of the church's previous split. He will never fully understand my endeavor of growing LFT in my way, and he will never have to break some of the barriers I had to break. However, I will never know what he had to sacrifice, let go of, and overcome. I will never know what it feels to pastor the 5,000 people he will pastor. I was the foundation of the ministry for 27 years, but now he has the tools to make it go even higher! He will raise LFT to levels I never could, and guess what? I'm good with that! My ministry is not about me! Pastor Tuck honors me in ways I never imagined a successor could honor his predecessor.

We have discussed two security (or should we say *insecurity*?) issues. Now, let's look at our ego problem. The question is, can you let go? I mean *really* let go. Can you allow the next person to carry out their mission without your input? Now, don't take that in the wrong way. Pastor Tuck and I have many conversations about the ministry, but it's never about what I think he should do. When he tells me his vision, I may give a suggestion or two; but at the end of the conversation, he knows I'm his biggest cheerleader.

My calling and mindset changed. I knew I had to find my successor in order for the church to continue growing. Now, I know who I am and what I brought to the table for Living Faith, and I am secure with that. I'm proud of the young man God raised up to continue a vision I would never have had. In order to let go, you have to swallow your pride, remove intimidation, and forget about what others will say.

Many asked me, "How does it make you feel when he tears down something you have built, or a design you created?" Honestly, it makes me feel good. Something leaps within me. He will not do everything right. Neither did I. Making mistakes is what makes us great. For every success, we have seven failures. The more we fail, the more we succeed. It makes me proud that my successor sees the next level I did not see. So he tears things down and reconstructs them to what they need to be!

When do you let go? After ten years? Twenty? Fifty? The sigmoid curve tells us that, in order to move something forward, we must make changes while things are still growing. There isn't a time limit, but here are a few pointers to help you know when to let go:

1. When you lose the vision
2. When others are growing faster than you
3. When you no longer enjoy what you're doing
4. When you're not willing to change, or do things you don't like to do
5. When a new generation is coming, and you only see the bad they do
6. When money is the only reason you stay
7. When you have more bad days than good ones
8. When it starts costing you your health or relationships
9. When you lose your connection with God

You can't move forward until you learn to let go! My favorite part of the movie *Frozen* is when Elsa sings "Let It Go." That is what we must do to have a successful succession. We can't run to the monkey bars while hanging onto the chains of the swing. Let it go. There's something else for you. Don't be intimidated. Allow God to promote you to your new place! That's what I did, and I can honestly tell you this: I love it, and so will you!

For Thought:

1. Have you ever jumped too soon? What was the result of your impatience?

2. What have you waited too long to do? What opportunities have passed you by?

3. What insecurities may hold you back from successful transition?

chapter 11

TAKING THE LEAP

HAT DOES IT TAKE TO TRANSITION? I think, by this point, we're all on the same page. It takes a leap of faith. Transition is never easy, and it gets even harder as we get older. I remember as a child when VCRs came out, and I swore I would never be like my outdated parents. With a VCR, all you had to do was put the television on the right channel, put the tape in the machine, and hit play. Anyone could do that—or so I thought.

As technology has rapidly moved forward in the twenty-first century, I've discovered that it's harder and harder for me to keep up. I'm not interested in the iPhone 10X. I'm perfectly fine with the iPhone 8 because I know where everything is. We moved from

DVDs to Netflix to movie channels to recording, and I can no longer operate the television with one remote—it takes three now! My millennial son still laughs when we need to watch a movie, because I have to call him to ask which remote to use and what to push. He busted out laughing when he came home last week and said, "Dad, you must have figured it out! You don't call anymore." Then, to my embarrassment, he turned over each of the remotes. There, on the back of each, was a yellow sticky note with instructions. We both laughed, but I dared him to remove it. All along, I thought I'd never turn into my parents; somehow along the way, I found myself unwilling to move forward.

"It is when we are in transition that we are most completely alive." —William Bridges

---

In order to transition, you have to learn to *jump*! You have to let go of the past to move to the improved future of your destiny. Imagine the first time someone said, "Hey, I moved the outhouse inside the house!" Can you imagine the resistance? "What about the smell? What about the flies? How could you put that nasty thing in the house where I live?" All because they had never seen it done that way. Let me remind you: if it ain't broke, maybe you ought to break it! There are still millions of ideas no one has imagined; millions of songs no one has written; millions of dreams yet to be fulfilled. Take a leap of faith and go for it!

What if Martin Luther King Jr. hadn't had a dream? Where would the push for equality be today? What if Abraham Lincoln had given up after losing so many times? What if Barack Obama had thrown in the towel when he was defeated in Congress in Illinois? What if you never take a leap?

Here's a better question: what if you do?

It's so easy to get comfortable where you are and live the rest of your life in complacency. No one was pushing me out of pastoring. In fact, I loved it. But I also knew there was another building project coming up and that I wasn't excited about it anymore. I knew there was more growth, but my desire had shifted. It would have been easy to ride it out ten more years to retirement, but what would have been the cost? The church I'd built and loved for so many years would have declined. I would have lost faith and confidence, as the calling shifted and I tried to continue doing things the old way. The cost would have been too high. Leaping in faith was scary and uncertain, but losing my vision was scarier. I knew the only way to go forward was to close my eyes and leap in the direction of my destiny.

I'm reminded of when I was 30. I went through a phase of daring myself, wanting to try things I'd never dreamed of trying. Maybe it was a pre-mid-life crisis. I considered some strange activities, especially for my conservative personality—feats such as getting a tattoo, or even a body piercing! When I look back at that time, I have to laugh. Perhaps I was trying to prove to myself that I wasn't your average, everyday pastor, husband, or father. In my life and ministry, I've been called many things, but never boring or predictable!

One item on my bucket list that I almost changed my mind about was skydiving. I've always been a fan of thrill rides, adventures, and new experiences. I was elated when I scheduled the big dive! My wife, on the other hand, didn't share my excitement. She didn't even ride with me to North Carolina to meet our friend, who was the skydiving instructor. She opted to stay home and wait by the phone to find out if I made it safely. I'm sure she was praying I would back out, or that an unpredicted thunderstorm would cancel the trip!

Suddenly, there I was on that crop duster, getting hooked into my gear and trying to hang onto every word my instructor said. I was all in, and so excited about this new adventure...until the other young lady and her guide got on the ledge to dive first! Suddenly, fear gripped me. All kinds of thoughts invaded my mind: What if I somehow broke away from my instructor? What if my parachute failed? Would I see my wife and sons again?

I told my instructor I was reconsidering the jump. He assured me it would be the most exhilarating thing I could ever experience. I asked him to honestly tell me if he was in any way suicidal. He told me he loved himself way too much to ever consider it, and the next thing I knew, there we were, standing on the edge of that aircraft. The only thing left to do was *take the leap!*

Skydiving was an awesome experience, and I'm glad I did it. But believe me: when I jumped, my faith wasn't in myself or my ability to land safely. Every bit of my trust was in my instructor! Without him, my day would have ended much differently!

It's the same way with life, ministry, business, and relationships. From time to time, you'll find it necessary to try something new and exciting that stretches and challenges you. Feel free to ask your questions. But take the training. Get suited up. Trust your wise, experienced instructor, and *take the leap of faith* so you can soar to new heights of destiny.

I've never doubted that leap once I made it. All the doubt came before the leap. Once I let go, I began to soar. My church soared higher, and my successor broke all boundaries. No, it's not easy. If it was, everyone would do it! Only the brave, that dare to reach greater heights and desire to achieve their purpose in life, will take the leap. Will you be one of them?

For Thought:

1. What's holding you hostage from leaping?

2. What would it take to empower you to jump?

3. What are you waiting for?

chapter 12

#LIVINGMYDREAM

ONLY 5 PERCENT OF AMERICANS living today actually achieve their dreams! Out of the 95 percent that remain, 87 percent have totally forgotten they even had a dream. Why is it that we quit dreaming? What so overwhelms us that we lose our childhood dreams? Many people have said to me, "If I had it to do over again, I would…"

While we can't change our past, we can change the final chapters in our life. As long as we're breathing, there's still time and space for us to dream again! Take a few minutes, and DOL: Dream Out Loud. You may be afraid to do this, thinking that people will laugh or mock your ideas. Remember, it's *your* dream—not theirs! What would it be like if you were living your dream to-day, and for the rest of your life? Indeed, that is the will of God for each of our lives! God never gives us a dream we can't accomplish. However, we have to find someone who believes in us enough to let us dream out loud, and assist us in fulfilling our purpose.

As I stated in the beginning of this book, I was extremely happy pastoring Living Faith Tabernacle. It was my dream, my passion, and my life! So many asked me why my dream has changed. I continue to reiterate that my dream did not die; God took me to a new level! It's humorous to me when people ask, "Don't you miss preaching?" The truth is that I'm preaching now more than ever! Doors of opportunity have opened for me to minister to churches I never would have visited as a senior pastor. My current position gives me the chance to minister to other congregations about how to care for God's shepherds, and how to care for their ministries from an outside perspective.

"When shifts and transitions shake you to the core, see that as a sign of greatness that's about to occur." —Anonymous

---

Now, when I walk through the airport, or down the aisles of the grocery store, people no longer call me by my name. Many people approach me and say, "Hey, you're '#LivingMyDream,' aren't you?" Most no longer know me as pastor, bishop or even professor. My new name has found me! I love being called "#LivingMyDream"! I believe so many people have been drawn to the name because it is their desire, as well.

Everyone wants to live their dream, but not many feel free to leap out in faith because they fear the unknown. I must admit, when I ventured out from what was familiar, the last thing I thought I'd be known for is "#LivingMyDream." I could see no way of fulfilling the goals in my life without being behind the pulpit as senior pastor. Little did I know, God was setting me up for my purpose. I've grown to realize I was not born to be a pastor, professor, or business owner, but to give hope to the hopeless! With this calling, I can be a pastor and give hope to my congregation. I can be a professor and give my students hope in the classroom. I can be a business owner and give entrepreneurs hope. I've grown to realize that, when you are living your dream, your dream will always make room for you.

Living your dream isn't common, and loving transition is even less common. However, you have to go through transition, one way or another. It's amazing to me that we don't fight certain transitions. We've all transitioned from LP albums to 8-track tapes. We moved from 8-tracks to cassettes, from cassettes to CDs, from CDs to thumb drives, and from thumb drives to satellite radio. Still, we struggle with the transition into our destiny. It's been said that society transitions every 3 years, while the church transitions every 30 years. Still, we want to do the same things and reap different results—that's known as insanity. Things do not change until we do.

I now realize that, had I not leaped, I wouldn't have met some very respected pastors, congregations, prayer mothers, politicians, global leaders, and dignitaries. Would my health have suffered? Would the church have suffered as it outgrew me? Would I have suffered as I outgrew it? Possibly, that entrepreneur would never have opened that business; that soul would never have come to the altar; that faith may never have been tested; and that miracle may never have happened. Therefore, when I look back, I'm thankful for every phase of my life; but I find myself even more thankful for where my future is taking me. There are still amazing platforms I haven't yet been on. There are amazing men and women I haven't met, and corporations that haven't yet been inspired. I am ready to transition into more of God's grace and favor.

As I conclude this book, I want to ask you once more: what will it take for you to truly live your dream? What makes you get up every morning? If money was no object and education wasn't a factor, what would you be doing this very moment? When you answer these simple questions, you begin to uncover your purpose. I challenge you to answer these questions right now.

What wakes you up in the morning? Prayerfully, I trust you didn't respond with, "The alarm clock," or "Because I have to go to work."

I can truly say that my dreams wake me up every morning! When you're fulfilling your dreams, it doesn't seem like work at all. I realize that many reading this book may think something like, "I can't afford to quit my job," or, "I can't afford to chase my dreams." Please understand, you only get one shot at life. What a sad ending it would be, indeed, if we left this earth and hadn't fulfilled the purpose for which God put us here.

What are you passionate about? What's the first step you can take today to start living your life on purpose? I promise that your dream will make provisions for you, and bring you joy in every moment of your life! I'm living my dream beyond measure, and it simply took the act of stepping out in faith and trusting God to fill in the blanks. I couldn't have dreamed of where God has me today. I never imagined He could move me out of my comfort zone and begin something new in me after 27 years. Even while I was faithful and happy, He allowed something new to be birthed in of me, and it was greater than what I had ever known.

Let me challenge you as you lay this book down—after you've contemplated the chapters, stories, and encouraging thoughts—to begin to live your dream. You don't have to wait another minute. In fact, you shouldn't! You should start planning the first step to living every day on purpose right now, so that you too can #LiveYourDream!

For Thought:

1. What is your dream?

2. What wakes you up each morning?

3. If money was not an object, and education was not a factor, what would you be doing right now?

ABOUT THE AUTHOR

*D*R. CHRISTOPHER BOWEN is Founder of Living Faith Tabernacles. He was born and raised in South Charleston, Ohio, then moved to Atlanta after graduating high school to attend Beulah Heights University. He received his Bachelor's degree there in 1987.

In 1990, Pastor Chris founded Living Faith Tabernacle in a small hotel room with 15 members. The ministry has grown at a phenomenal rate and after the seventh building project, the sanctuary on Old Dixie Highway in Forest Park, Georgia now seats 1,300 people. The church hosts an 8AM and 11AM service each Sunday and holds weekly Bible studies and youth services on Wednesdays.

Dr. Bowen continued his education, receiving his Master's degree in Leadership Development at Southwestern Christian University in Oklahoma City,

Oklahoma and his Doctorate of Ministry in Pastoral Care and Counseling from Oral Roberts University in April 2011. Dr. Bowen is a full time professor at Beulah Heights University, where he instructs both Success for Life and Marriage and Family classes. He is the Director of Dream Releaser Coaching, a motivational speaker, and travels internationally to speak on topics such as time management, body language comunication, and financial freedom. In addition to operating in leadership of ministries, he is also a business owner and entrepreneur.

In 2017, Dr. Bowen felt the pull of God to venture into other areas od traveling ministry. He passed the mantle of Senior Pastor of LFT to Pastor Jeremy Tuck. Dr. Bowen feels that although his time as senior pastor is over that his life in ministry is far from done.

Dr. Bowen has authored many books. His newest release is entitled, *Beyond Five Star Quality.* In this book, he informs us how to provide greater excellence and service to our personal and business lives, businesses, and or churches. Dr. Bowen resides in Jonesboro, Georgia, with his wife, Kathy. He is the proud father of two sons, and is a first time grandfather.

Dr. Chris Bowen · 678·409·0010 · DrChrisBowen@gmail.com

five star · executive development · motivational speaking · mentoring · consulting · coaching

LIFE COACHING & CERTIFICATION

Only 5% of the population ever live out their dreams? Many people go through life without even setting a goal, so they have no "destiny" to reach in their life. We coach and train coaches to live out their fullest potential.

TIME MANAGEMENT & PRODUCTIVITY

Business and life bring complications that can often make us feel stuck and unable to move forward. Managing time is critical to productivity and profitability. We specialize in empowering individuals and teams to reach their productivity goals and aspirations.

FINANCIAL FREEDOM & WEALTH BUILDING

Wealth building and financial freedom are goals that most people share. However, without the proper keys, you will roam in circles attempting to find a solution that helps you become continuously profitable, and consecutively successful for a richer future.

EXECUTIVE COACHING & MENTORING

Mentorship builds character for leaders. Leaders without mentors are leaving themselves vulnerable to unforeseen challenges that their organizations will face. Do you have the key tools to weather any storm?

LET'S CONNECT:

5 Star Personal and Corporate Development
Dr. Chris Bowen
1854 Spivey Village CR
Jonesboro, GA 30236

678-409-0010
DrChrisBowen@gmail.com
http://www.drchrisbowen.com